The Morning Quiet Time

Jack Winslow

Foreword by Philip Boobbyer

Published 2005 by John Faber,
2 Batworth Park House,
Crossbush,
Arundel, BN18 9PG.
johnfaber@tiscali.co.uk

in association with Initiatives of Change,
24 Greencoat Place,
London SW1P 1RD

ISBN 1 85239 035 2

Book design: Blair Cummock
Cover design: John Munro

Originally published in 1938, entitled *When I Awake*
by Hodder and Stoughton, London.
This new edition contains some small changes.

Printed by Ashford Colour Press, Gosport, Hampshire, UK

Contents

Foreword

Many people hunger for a closer walk with God. Yet, the practicalities can seem elusive. How does one actually get in touch with God and deepen one's spiritual life? Some people answer these questions by setting aside time for prayer each morning to seek inspiration for the day ahead. Yet it is not always easy to make a time of spiritual meditation fruitful. What does one actually do in a 'quiet time'? This book is a practical introduction to the subject.

Jack Winslow (1882-1974) was educated at Eton and Balliol College, Oxford. He was ordained as an Anglican minister in 1907 and became a lecturer at St Augustine's College in Canterbury in 1911. In 1914, he went as a missionary to India, where he spent the next twenty years. In 1921 he founded the Christa Seva Sangha Ashram, which was a place where Indian and English Christians of different castes and class origins could live together and share a life of poverty and service.

While in India, Winslow came under the influence of the Oxford Group (now called Initiatives of Change), which was initiated by the American Frank Buchman, and on returning to Britain he was active in Buchman's work.

Winslow's interest in community living, so evident during his time in India, continued after the war. In 1945, while he was Chaplain of Bryanston School in Dorset, he became a Trustee of Lee Abbey, a new Christian community centre in North Devon, and in 1948 he moved to Lee Abbey as Senior Chaplain, remaining there until 1962 when he retired.

The Morning Quiet Time, originally published in 1938 under the title *When I Awake*, reflected Winslow's own experience of prayer and meditation. As he says in the book, Winslow was first challenged to take quiet times seriously by the American religious leader and ecumenical pioneer, John R Mott. The Oxford Group, which challenged people to wait upon God in expectation of 'guidance', also shaped Winslow's understanding of what he here calls the 'the prayer of attention'.

At the same time, Winslow's religious thinking was shaped by India as well as the West. In his original introduction to *The Morning Quiet Time*, Winslow described the Indian mystical tradition as 'an immense enrichment' to his spiritual life; indeed, he had earlier published a book entitled *The Indian Mystic: some thoughts on India's contribution to Christianity* (1926). He clearly believed that it was possible to draw inspiration from the Eastern religious traditions while remaining true to his Christian beliefs.

Winslow was a warm and sympathetic person with a gift for pastoral care, and he often found himself needing to explain what a morning quiet time could involve. The result was this book. In his introduction, Winslow wrote:

> This book aims, however imperfectly, at meeting a very practical need. I am constantly asked to give, or find myself needing to give, simple instruction about how to keep what some call a 'quiet time' and others a 'morning watch' with God. I try to tell them as well as I can out of my experience, but I have felt the need of a book which could cover a rather wide ground within a reasonably small compass, and treat the matter simply enough for people not far advanced in the spiritual life. . . .
>
> There is in this book nothing recondite or learned; nor is there any attempt to guide those who are able to climb to the more exalted heights of the prayer life. . . . This is a simple book for simple people.

The Morning Quiet Time certainly has much to offer people who are setting out on a life of faith. At the same time, readers who have been walking a spiritual road for many years may also find inspiration in it.

In his epilogue, Winslow emphasises that the quiet time should not involve a retreat from the world so much as a deeper engagement with it. In thinking that reflects the ideas of the Oxford Group, he states that people who have a close touch with God possess the secret of security and inner peace that the world so much needs. Winslow suggests that when people listen to God, they could begin to see an end to fear, hatred, antagonism and war;

indeed he dares to foresee the dawning of a new world order itself.

Winslow would be the first to say that there are many ways of structuring a quiet time, and that the Spirit of God should be the ultimate guide. At the same time, people often need a framework with which to start or re-start their spiritual journey. This book can help to provide that.

Philip Boobbyer
School of History, University of Kent, UK
February 2005

God be in my head,
And in my understanding.

God be in my eyes,
And in my looking.

God be in my mouth,
And in my speaking.

God be in my heart,
And in my thinking.

God be at my end,
And at my departing.

The Morning Watch

DURING my time at Oxford as an undergraduate, John R Mott, then a young man, came to conduct a mission to the University. The week left a lasting impression on my life. It was not that the mission brought me any decisive religious experience. My concern with religion as the central interest of life had begun earlier, and my more vivid apprehension of Christ came later. But, amid much else that has been forgotten, one sentence spoken by Mott proved revolutionary. He said something of this kind: 'If you wish to make your life effective and useful for God and your fellow-men, it is essential that you should put aside unhurried time every day for a morning watch with God.'

Till that time I had been in the habit, from childhood onwards, of saying my morning prayers; but they had been little more than an expansion of the prayers of childhood, and had not occupied, I suppose, more than five or ten minutes. Though they helped me to remember God at the beginning of every day, they did not exercise any notable influence over my daily life. But now I caught a vision of something larger, more potent, more deeply formative in its effects. I saw that I must be prepared to keep at least half an hour, day by day, for this 'morn-

9

ing watch'. I saw that it must be something much more than 'saying prayers'. There must be in it some vital touch with the living God.

I began to learn something about the devotional study of the Bible, and to realise that through it one could receive, as it were, a personal message from God. I discovered that a good deal of self-discipline was needed if I were to rise early enough to keep this time with God and persevere regularly in it, and that this discipline in itself was salutary. And I found that, as I began to form this habit and continue in it, it did in fact begin to give a new tone and colour to life, and to exercise upon me the profound influence which John Mott had foretold.

Since those days I have never entirely abandoned the habit of a morning quiet time. I have often grown careless about it. For long spells I have allowed it to become hurried and formal, or given it inadequate time. But I have continued the practice of it; and, as life has gone on, and responsibilities have increased, I have realised more and more its vital necessity and increased the time spent upon it. And, looking back over the thirty-five years since that mission at Oxford, I can now say confidently that, if in these years I have been able to accomplish any useful service to God or man, I owe it to no other single cause so much as to the habit then started of keeping the morning watch.

My experience over these years has taught me that this quiet hour spent with God day by day is an unfailing secret of power, progress, purpose, and peace. It is an ever fresh spring of power. Over and over again I have risen at the beginning of a new day feeling utterly inadequate for the tasks awaiting me, tired in body, dull in mind, and defeated in spirit; but the renewal, in the quiet, of touch with the living God has recreated me and restored my energies, physical, mental and spiritual. I have experienced the truth of Archbishop Trench's lines:

Lord, what a change within us one short hour
Spent in Thy presence can prevail to make!
What heavy burdens from the weary take!
What parched grounds refresh, as with a shower!
. . . .
We kneel, how weak! We rise, how full of power!

A striking illustration of this transmission of power, which I heard nearly thirty years ago, has always remained with me. During a mission at Wimbledon, when I was curate there, we were holding an open-air service in a crowded street, and the missioner was speaking about prayer, when a tram passed by and for the moment drowned his voice. As it receded in the distance, he pointed to it and said: 'Look how swiftly and easily it speeds on its way when it lifts its arm to the live wire above! And how powerless it is to move an inch without that vital contact!'

If we want power in our own lives—victory over the things that get us down, and the invigorating sense of adequacy for any tasks or situations that await us through the day— we must let the Spirit of God recharge us morning by morning. If we want power for the lives of others—power to help, cheer, direct, change them—we must attend still more to the daily replenishment of our own supply. If I find myself at any time out of power, with no message or effective help for others, it is nearly always because at some point or other I have lost vital touch with God.

The morning quiet time with God is also the surest guarantee of progress. In the Christian life there can be no standing still. Failure to go forward invariably means going back. If I appear to stand exactly where I did a year ago, it must mean that I have been missing all those new things which God was waiting to teach and give me. In my own experience this kind of stagnation is most often due to the fact that my quiet times with God have become formal or uncreative.

On the other hand, if I can really say with the prophet, 'Morning by morning He wakeneth mine ear to hear as they that are taught,' (*Isaiah* 50: 4) then I find that I begin at once to go forward. I grow in understanding of God as I meditate on the Bible. I get fresh glimpses of His character, His purposes, the ways of His working. I grow in understanding of myself and my fellow-men, and of the ways of helping them. I grow in my own spiritual life. There are fewer points where I find myself defeated. There is greater alertness to the guidance of God. In all such times there is a sense of advance and of adventure, of new heights to scale, new worlds to win. If we would go 'from strength to strength' in the Christian life, we must begin each day by unhurried time with God.

The keeping of the morning watch fills life with

purpose. I shall have more to say of this in detail when I write about the prayer of attention. But I may say here that, since I learnt morning by morning to commit the day to God, to try to see His plan for each day so far as He chose to show it, and to wait for whatever orders He might wish to give me, life has had for me a thrill and a purpose such as it never had before.

I realise that every day I have assigned to me some part, however insignificant, in God's great campaign. Things which before seemed unimportant— the writing of letters, conversations, 'chance' meetings—become filled with meaning, and I see how each day, and each hour of the day, may be creative for God. There is then no room for boredom over a multitude of common-place jobs, and none of the old sense of futility or drift, since all the tasks of the day are woven into the one design.

The quiet hour with God in the early morning is also a sure secret of inward peace. This, too, I have tested constantly in my own experience. I have risen from bed with a sense of anxiety or worry— perhaps troubled about definite problems for which I could see no solution; perhaps haunted by that vague sense of depression about nothing in particular which so many experience in the early morning. I have entered on my quiet tryst with God, and in the stillness, as I have committed myself with all my anxieties to God, peace has stolen back into my soul.

Sometimes it has happened that quite suddenly the clouds of worry or depression have rolled away, and the sun has once more shone out from a clear sky.

Sometimes these clouds have only gradually been dispersed, but by the time the quiet hour is over, all is bright. Sometimes the clouds have not passed; the problems and difficulties are still unsolved; but the sense of the burden of them is removed. The way out has not been shown, but there has come the peace of knowing that God has all in hand, and is bearing the burden Himself, so what cause is left for worry? This sense of peace in the heart of the storm is perhaps the most wonderful of all. It is essentially that peace, of which our Lord on the very verge of all His sufferings said to His disciples: 'Peace I leave with you: my peace I give unto you; not as the world giveth give I unto you.'

It is important to remember that times of spiritual aridity, when we have little 'sensible' realisation (viz. realisation in feeling) of God's presence and peace, are not necessarily the result of sin. They may, of course, be so; and, if we are experiencing such times, we must ask God to show us whether they are due to some fault in ourselves which needs to be dealt with. But all the masters of the spiritual life tell us that such dryness is not in itself sinful, and that, so far from being a hindrance to spiritual growth, can, if rightly used, be a special aid to it. To continue in prayer with steadfast discipline, without the help of conscious realisation, strengthens our wills and gives us really a surer hold on God than we had before. Some of the great saints have had constant times of spiritual aridity. The 'sensible' experience of God is not ours to command. The recollection of this will save us, on the one hand, from self-congratulation when we have it, and, on the other, from discouragement when it is lacking.

Often in India, as we have sat on the ground in the open air for our worship in the still hour of morning twilight before the sunrise, or again in the evening, facing the fading glory of the sunset sky, I have known the soothing benediction of this peace. Quietly we have sat, for fifteen or twenty minutes, with no spoken prayer or word, drinking in the very peace of God for frayed nerves, tired bodies, or anxious minds. The time of silence has closed with the Indian benediction: '*shanti, shanti, shanti*,' 'peace, peace, peace'; and the words have seemed to echo the very heart of the inward experience of that quiet hour.

The stress on this watch with God as the *morning* watch is of vital importance. Actually what the Psalmist says is: 'My soul fleeth unto the Lord *before* the morning watch.' And it is indeed the *early* morning which is the time we should keep sacred to prayer. No other time takes the place of this.

It is the time when we are most free from distractions. The sleep of the night has come between us and the cares and work of the previous day, and the work of the new day has not yet started. We can give ourselves without fear of interruption to this one supreme task of prayer.

The early morning is also the time when our minds should be at their freshest. I know that some people complain that this is not so, but the reason is usually that either they are getting insufficient time for sleep, or owing to some physical or mental cause their sleep is broken and troubled. Till this cause is dealt with, what I write will not apply to them. Those in normal health, however, wake from sound refreshing sleep renewed in body and mind, their faculties restored to full vigour for the work of another day. The time with God on which the quality of that day will depend should claim their first freshness.

But there is a reason deeper than either of these for consecrating these waking moments to the quiet time with God. There is something in our psychological make-up which makes us peculiarly susceptible to deeper intuitions in our first minutes of re-awakened consciousness. Most people must have had the experience of going to sleep with some problem on which they have expended long thought still unsolved, and waking in the morning with the solution in mind. Something has happened during the hours of unconsciousness in the deeper levels of the mind which has released the truth or the memory which conscious thinking or effort could not reach and may even have entangled further.

We have much yet to learn about the full significance and purpose of sleep. We know how essential it is for the renewal of our bodily and mental faculties. The psychologists have explored the meaning of our dreams and made full use of them in the work of restoring mental health. But we have not fully realised how much the hours of sleep may mean for *spiritual* renewal and enlightenment. There is a striking thought of the Psalmist which is lost in our Prayer Book rendering. He says: 'He giveth unto his beloved in sleep.' (*Psalm* 128: 2)

This treasure given in sleep we may garner in our waking moments. In one sense our morning quiet time should begin in fact overnight. We should fall asleep with God in our last thoughts, with the desire that we may spend the night with Him, and that, while our conscious minds take their rest, our unconscious minds may be open to His influence and teaching. As the old hymn has it:

> *Let but the eyes due slumber take,*
> *The soul to Thee be aye awake.*

Then we shall wake already expectant and eager to gather up what He has been giving in sleep, and what He will give further in the freshness of that early morning hour.

These things together help us to understand why the men and women whose lives have been most richly used for God and His Kingdom have always risen early in the morning to have ample time for starting the day with God. To take only three examples:

John Wesley, whose work changed the face of England, was always at prayer in the early hours of the morning before others were stirring. Mahatma Gandhi, who swayed the multitudes of India with almost miraculous power, rose at four o'clock for his time of silent meditation and prayer to God. Frank Buchman, to whom under God the Oxford Group owes its origin, often testified to the fact that his main inspiration was drawn from those early hours of the day in which he listened in quiet to hear the voice of the living God. And one of the chief secrets of the power of the Group has been the stress laid on the vital importance of the quiet time with God in the first hour of the day.

Innumerable examples could be cited from the history of great spiritual leaders, showing how the morning watch with God was the constant secret of their effectiveness and strength.

No doubt the discipline required for rising early enough for this unhurried time with God is for a while hard; but the matter is of such vital importance for our entire life that no effort can be too costly to this end; and once the habit is established it is maintained without much difficulty. Soldiers are expected to be out on parade at whatever hour of the morning is ordered, and hardly look to the sergeant-major to congratulate them if they are present and punctual!

Yet we, engaged on a supreme campaign in God's army at a time of critical emergency, so readily complain of being asked to leave our beds an hour earlier than our work demands, or yield to self-congratulation if we succeed. Let us once and for all, in sheer shame, banish such luke-warmness and indiscipline, if we are guilty of it, and for this most important of all tasks brace ourselves to 'endure hardness as good soldiers of Jesus Christ'.

Entering into Stillness

WE pass on now to consider how to use the time which we set aside for our morning quiet time with God.

The *length* of this time each must decide for himself. For my own part I have found that I cannot now do with less than an hour, and I prefer to have it, if possible, in one unbroken stretch. But people's circumstances differ, and a man who has to be very early at work, or a woman who has to get children dressed, fed, and sent to school may find this scarcely feasible. Such may shorten the early morning time by reserving their meditation on the Bible, for instance, or their intercessions, or both, till later. But I am sure that, for the reasons already given, it is better to have the whole hour at the beginning of the day; and often some rearrangement of duties can be found to make this possible. Where there's a will, there's a way.

Each must also decide, in the light of his own experience, how in detail he will spend the time, and what order the different parts of his prayer-time will follow. For myself, I prefer to keep flexible, and both the contents and order of my morning watch vary from time to time. But there are certain essential elements which should find a place always in our quiet hour,

19

and it is with these that I shall deal in the following chapters, in the order which I usually follow myself.

First, then, we should spend a few moments in entering into stillness, that body, mind and spirit may be prepared for this which we are about to do.

Stillness of body

This may seem a small matter, yet it is of real importance. There are many people whose lives are passed in one continuous rush. From morning till evening they are never quiet. Often their nerves are jaded and overwrought. They need to learn the habit of relaxing their bodies completely, from time to time, if they would get the mind at rest.

Indian spiritual teachers, who have developed the practice of contemplation to an exact science far beyond us of the West, lay great stress on this preparation of the body. They prescribe for it a posture which will combine *rest* and *attention*. On the one hand we must be able so to forget our bodies that they shall in no way hinder our prayer. There must be, therefore, complete relaxation. On the other hand, this relaxation must not be such as will conduce to sleep, but must be combined with an alert awareness.

The Indian teachers also lay great stress on deep, regular breathing, and there is no doubt that this does also conduce to quietness and health of body and mind. It is worth stating here that some physical exercises on arising, including deep breathing exercises, help to banish sleepiness and to give freshness, alertness and poise.

Stillness of mind

We must empty our minds of all outside distractions and hold them ready for prayer. 'Wheresoever the fickle and unsteady mind wanders off, there shall he check it and bring it into obedience to the spirit.' In another place it is said that the mind is at first like a monkey, jumping hither and thither from bough to bough; and no one who has tried to practise the prayer of quiet will question the truth of the comparison. As it says in the *Bhagavadgita*, we must persevere: 'Little by little he shall win stillness by steady control of the mind.'

St Teresa compares this gradual recollection of the mind with the way in which a swarm of bees buzzing around the hive are slowly gathered within it and settle to rest.

I know that this question of stillness of mind constitutes a difficulty to many who wish to pray better. They find it so hard to concentrate. One thing I would say to them is: When your thoughts wander, don't get fussed and bothered, for this only makes things worse; but quietly each time bring them back to the point of attention. The habit of concentrating quickly grows with practice. Learn it in the ordinary work of life, and you will find it available in your prayer time.

I have myself found that attention to prayer is greatly assisted by speaking aloud to God. I think of Him as with me, close at hand; and often I speak out my thoughts to Him quite simply, as I would speak to a friend. I find that it makes Him real, and my thoughts no longer wander.

Stillness of spirit

We must not only be quiet in body and mind but still our spirits before the great All-Wise, All-Holy, and All-Loving God, into Whose presence we come. There is a restlessness of spirit, corresponding to the restlessness of mind and body, which makes prayer impossible. I find it is generally due, in my own case, to my own feelings and desires and needs looming too large. My own busy little ego has to pass into the background before I can properly attend to God.

This interference of the busy, fussy self with our prayers has been strikingly pictured by the Indian poet, Rabindranath Tagore, in one of his songs. He speaks of coming to his tryst with God 'in the silent dark', but another follows him whom he tries in vain to escape.

> *He makes the dust rise from the earth with his*
> *swagger:*
> *He adds his loud voice to every word that I utter.*
> *He is my own little self, my Lord, he knows*
> *no shame; but I am ashamed to come to*
> *Thy door in his company.*

How can we get rid of this swaggering little self and attain the stillness of spirit we need for prayer ? Only as we commit ourselves and our whole prayer time into the charge of the Holy Spirit Himself. 'We know not how to pray as we ought,' (*Romans* 8: 26) but the Holy Spirit, Who 'makes intercession for us', will also pray in us and through us, if we will let Him. It has made the greatest difference to my own prayers since I realised this. Formerly there was a certain strain and tenseness, as though the whole burden of praying aright rested upon me. Now that I commit my time of quiet to the Holy Spirit, He is the Inspirer and Leader in prayer, and I have only to cooperate with Him. I believe this practice of inviting the Holy Spirit to pray in us is of real importance in the devotional life.

In the power of the Holy Spirit, then, we rest in stillness before Almighty God, our Father. We leave, for the present, all thought of ourselves and our own needs. Our spirit bows in humble and thankful adoration before our Creator, as we lift our hymn in unison with the choirs of heaven:

> *Holy, Holy, Holy;*
> *Lord God Almighty;*
> *Heaven and Earth are full of Thy glory,*
> *Glory be to Thee,*
> *O Lord, most High!*

Praise and Thanksgiving

OUR opening moments of silent adoration pass into praise and thanksgiving. We praise God for all that He is in Himself. We thank Him for all that He has done, is doing, and will do.

Praise and thanksgiving spring from the welling up within us of joy. They are its natural and overflowing expression. Joy stands second only to love among those nine characteristic qualities of the Christian character which make up, in St Paul's phrase, 'the fruit of the Spirit'.

When a man has come into new life through the Spirit, there springs up in him, first and foremost, a new love of God and his fellow-men, breaking through the old selfishness and transforming his whole outlook. This new-found love brings with it a quite extraordinary happiness—a happiness independent of outward circumstance. It is, in its deepest roots, joy in God, newly discovered and growing daily more wonderful; the sheer delight of the child in having such a marvellous father. But, springing from this source, it permeates every activity of life and every relationship.

The true Christian is radiantly happy—not because he has no troubles, temptations or difficulties (for of these he has his full share), but because he is known and loved by God, lives for His service, and has all his security in Him. This is the joy Christ promised, which 'No man taketh from you.'

This joy breaks out in praise and thanksgiving. It cannot be restrained from finding expression. All life becomes for the Christian a psalm of praise—'Whatsoever ye do in word or deed, do all in the name of the Lord Jesus, giving thanks to God the Father through Him.' (*Colossians* 3: 17)

It is fitting, therefore, and indeed inevitable, that praise and thanksgiving should take their place in the forefront of our morning prayers. Our joy in God breaks out with each new day's beginning. His mercies are 'new every morning'.

So spontaneous ought this praise and thanksgiving to be that it will need no marshalling or direction. Gushing forth from an inexhaustible spring of joy, it will create for itself the channels in which to flow. But actually most of us fall, all too frequently, below this level of overflowing praise; and for such people, at such times, there is value in some regular scheme or method of devotion.

My own practice is to have a scheme of praise and thanksgiving, which I may use if the Spirit moves me, and do often use over a prolonged period. On the other hand I feel free to discard it, if I am moved to more spontaneous expression of joy.

It may be of help to some if I give here one such scheme, not so much with a view to its being adopted entire, as in the hope that it may help others in preparing their own. The scheme covers a week, starting with Monday, and working up to its climax on Sunday, the great day of praise.

Monday: Praise of God in His own eternal Being, the self-existent One, the great I Am, the Trinity in unity.

Thanksgiving for the complete security of the life rooted in Him, and that the future, like the past and present, is in His keeping.

Tuesday: Praise of God the Creator, infinite in wisdom; the uncreated beauty at the heart of all things.

Thanksgiving for creation; the marvel and the loveliness of this universe in which we live; the power to see and wonder, to enjoy and to praise.

Wednesday: Praise of God the Father, watching over all His children in His divine providence; unchanging love.

Thanksgiving for all that God's loving providence has done for me from earliest childhood to this present time; for all the simple joys of daily life in the home.

Thursday: Praise of God Incarnate in Jesus; His birth; His life of selfless service; His teaching; His revelation of God.

Thanksgiving for His continued working through His body, the Church; and for the Church's worship and sacraments, particularly the Holy Communion of His body and blood.

Friday: Praise of Christ crucified for us, the one perfect sacrifice of love; 'the Lamb of God that taketh away the sin of the world.'

Thanksgiving for all that has sprung from the Cross; for the Cross in our own lives; for the darknesses and difficulties of life, by which we learn and grow.

Saturday: Praise of God for His apostles, martyrs, and all saints who have followed the way of Christ crucified.

Thanksgiving for saints in common life; for those we have known and loved, who rest in Paradise.

Sunday: Praise of Christ risen and exalted, and of the Holy Spirit sent forth at Pentecost.

Thanksgiving for new birth; for life in the Spirit; for the spread of the Kingdom of Christ throughout the world.

These subjects are given in the briefest outline, and are capable of almost unlimited expansion. Even so there are multitudes of subjects for praise and thanksgiving which they do not cover. Also we shall desire to thank God for the particular mercies He is constantly bestowing on us; but this we shall do best, not in the morning, but as we look back evening by evening over the past day. For my own part I have been amazed, time after time, as I review at night time what has seemed in its passing to be a normal day of no outstanding interest, to find how many evidences it contains of God's love, how many causes to thank Him.

The habit of praise not only springs out of joy, but also in turn deepens it. Thanksgiving is the surest cure of depression. The devils of worry, fear and gloom can find only the most fleeting lodging place in a mind that is constantly thanking God.

This, however, is only a happy by-product of thanksgiving. It would destroy itself if it became its motive. I offer praise and thanks to God, not for anything that I may gain by it, but because He is good beyond all telling, and He is mine and I am His.

Adoration, worship, praise, thanksgiving— these are the highest activities of which man is capable, and they are not learnt in a day, nor indeed in a lifetime. Yet we may be learning to offer them better all our life through, and so have our share here, however tiny and imperfect, in the unceasing worship of heaven.

The Daily Surrender

FROM praise and thanksgiving we pass to the renewal, day by day, of our self-surrender to God.

I use the word 'surrender' as being on the whole that which best expresses our complete self-giving to God. But we must always remember that the surrender of our wills to God is not an act of weakness or one involving any loss of individuality but, on the contrary, is the one way by which our wills attain their true freedom and all our particular gifts and powers their fullest development.

Hitherto following the order of our Lord's pattern prayer we have turned our thoughts away from ourselves to God Himself. Now we return to ourselves; but even so it is not as yet in order to ask anything for ourselves, but so to give ourselves to Him that through us His name may be hallowed, His Kingdom hastened, and His Will done. We are still within the first half of the Lord's Prayer.

It is natural that the renewal of our surrender should follow thanksgiving for it is the best form that thanksgiving can take.

'We beseech Thee give us that due sense of all Thy mercies, that our hearts may be unfeignedly thankful, and that we show forth Thy praise, not only with our lips but in our lives, by giving up ourselves to Thy service.' All the goodness of God to us demands that we give ourselves completely to Him in return.

This daily self-surrender to God is an essential part of Christian living. It carries continually forward that which begins at our conversion or change. It takes for granted this initial step—that we have realised the absolute claim upon us of the love of God, as it is revealed in Christ, and that we have given ourselves over, body, mind and spirit, to Him, facing the cost of total obedience, and entering into the glorious liberty and happiness and new life of His children.

If there has not been this great initial surrender, the daily surrender can have no meaning. If we have never really asked God to take complete charge of our lives, facing honestly every sin of which we are conscious, making such restitution as He shows us is required, and putting all that we have and are at His disposal; then it is a mockery to make an act of daily surrender.

But if we have faced the whole cost of a life totally committed to God, and accepted the challenge, and found a new birth into freedom and victory, then it is essential that our surrender be daily renewed. Otherwise we shall soon fall back to the old levels.

Sometimes in movements of revival this has happened. Under the impulse of the first wonderful new experience of God's reality and power, the chains of sin have been broken, a thrilling sense of release and joy has come, and all life seems to have been permanently changed.

A few months later, not only has this first warm glow passed away but old temptations have begun to resume their sway, and the high hopes of victorious living have faded. What is the reason? In my own experience there are three main reasons for this falling back. Sometimes it is due to the lack of Christian fellowship. The novice in the spiritual life finds no one to direct and help him along the new road on which he has started. In other cases it is due to lack of 'exercise'.

The new life, if it is to grow, must find active self-expression in service and witness to others. Best of all is it when these two elements of fellowship and active work can be combined, and the man whose life has been changed by the Spirit of God finds himself one of a company of people similarly changed who are engaged in team work together, passing on to others what they have received.

But there is a third reason for falling away, perhaps the commonest of all; and that is, that the man whose life has been transformed by the power of God in answer to his surrender has never learnt the necessity of renewing this surrender every morning. He has looked on that which happened at his conversion as happening once for all. He has not realised that he must 'daily increase in God's Holy Spirit more and more,' and that this can only happen if he allows that Holy Spirit to penetrate his life more and more deeply day by day.

The daily surrender is essential to spiritual

growth. It is the way by which we give God more and more completely the freedom of our whole personality, and become increasingly available and usable for His Kingdom.

Sometimes, as we come in this morning quiet in silent adoration before the holiness of God, the Spirit convicts us afresh of sin, as He convicted Isaiah in the Temple when he saw the vision of the Holy One. There may be particular sins, unrealised before, which He shows us. In my own experience, convictions of sin come not so much through introspection, through laborious efforts of self-examination, as through a heightened experience of God's reality and holiness, in the light of which my own sins stand glaringly revealed.

Every such conviction is a call to further surrender. So far from being an occasion for getting depressed at our little progress, it is a call to thank God that the Holy Spirit is at work in us, dealing with all that is unsound in the hidden roots of our life. As we see some new sin we confess it humbly to God with prayer for His forgiveness and resolve also, if humility or honesty demand it, to confess it to our friends. Then out of our very failure comes a new advance and through a fresh surrender God enters into a more complete control of our lives.

But whether there be definite convictions of sin or not, we renew our surrender to God in this morning quiet. The words may be of the simplest: 'Here am I, Lord, at your service for the work of another day'— or some may prefer to make a fuller act, surrendering body, mind, spirit, will; all that we have and all that we are; time, talents, friendships, possessions, and the rest to God. Or in the words of an old hymn:

> *Lord, I my vows to Thee renew;*
> *Scatter my sin as morning dew;*
> *Guard my first springs of thought and will,*
> *And with Thyself my spirit fill.*
>
> *Direct, control, suggest, this day,*
> *All I design or do or say,*
> *That all my powers with all their might*
> *In Thy sole glory may unite.*

It is not the words that matter. There may be no words at all. It is not the feelings that matter. The act may be quite unemotional—is perhaps better thus. What matters is the simple act of will by which we once again yield ourselves completely to the Divine Will, that God may direct and use us all the day through.

This it is, since He will never force us, which makes us available to Him.

This it is, as we shall see presently, which makes it possible for us to receive His orders.

This it is which opens the way for each day to become a creative day for God and His Kingdom.

Intercession

I think it is right to insert a chapter at this point on the subject of intercession. It is true that some people reserve the main part of their intercessions for some other time of day, e.g. mid-day or evening: and this is a perfectly legitimate practice. But our morning watch could hardly be complete without some measure of prayer for others and this small book would certainly be incomplete if it ignored intercessory prayer altogether.

My own usual practice is to restrict my early morning intercessions to *people* for whom I wish to pray, and it is a part of the morning watch that I would not on any account let go. This daily remembrance before God of a certain number out of a large and ever increasing circle of friends is the most wonderful and sure bond of friendship. It keeps fresh and vital the relationship with many whom one is seldom or never able to meet, and only rarely able to correspond with. In that moment when each individual is lifted up before God in prayer they are called to mind in the best possible way, and the tie of affection and mutual help is strengthened.

As a rule I offer these intercessions immediately after the renewal of my self-surrender. My thought is that, having offered myself afresh to God for His service, I then offer with myself those whom I desire specially to bring before Him that day. He knows their needs, bodily, mental, spiritual, in a way that I cannot. He has His perfect plan for each. I have only to bring them in thought before Him as the man sick of the palsy was brought by his friends to Jesus, with the desire that His will should be done for each one of them in its fullness.

I am convinced that we have in such prayer an instrument of tremendous power for helping others; and for winning people to God. This is not the place to speak of *corporate* intercession, the prayer of the 'two or three' gathered in Christ's Name, which has still greater effect. But the fervent prayer of the individual who has just consecrated himself afresh to God for his brethren's sake 'availeth much'. (*James* 5:16)

Those who have read the letters of the Cambridge University lecturer and college chaplain Forbes Robinson will remember how often he wrote about this power of prayer. He discovered in experience that he could often do more good to some undergraduate whom he was trying to help by half an hour's prayer for him than by half an hour's conversation with him.

I know I have not myself explored half sufficiently yet the unbounded possibilities of this earnest and sustained prayer for those whom I am seeking to help or win for God. I think there are some who can at first be reached in no other way; and, even when we are finding some particular person responsive, we may be sure that, unless we are praying for him as well as speaking with him, our work for him will be shallow and incomplete.

Once again, such intercession has great effect for the healing of those who are sick in mind or body. There is no need to stress this point. Probably almost all the readers of this book will be able to supply ample illustrations from their own experience of how 'the prayer of faith' does indeed 'heal the sick'.

Never have I experienced this more consistently than in the monthly service conducted for some years by Mr Madge and myself in India. Healing went forth in the name of Christ, not only to those who were brought there for the laying on of hands, but to those unable to be present, for whom we prayed; and each month's service included a long list of thanksgivings from those whose sufferings had been relieved or cured by the power of faithful prayer. This, again, was corporate prayer; but the individual prayer also produces wonderful results.

Is it possible to understand anything of the spiritual or psychological laws which underlie such help or healing as is undoubtedly given through prayer? Multiplied experience leaves us no room to doubt the *fact*, but might not some insight into the 'how' of intercession strengthen our faith in praying.

I should like, in answer, to pass on to others a line of thought which I have myself found helpful, and which I owe to my old London vicar and friend, H P Cronshaw. He used to put it to us like this: God respects our freedom, and will never force His blessings upon us. His power or help or healing can only go out where He finds some real response of faith and sympathy. Even in our own experience we know how powerless we are to help a man from whom we can win no kind of sympathetic response, who opposes to our attempts at friendship a blank wall of indifference. So even our Lord Himself could in His own village 'do no mighty work because of their unbelief'. There was no response of faith.

But there is such a thing as *vicarious* faith, which may play its part where the faith of the person chiefly concerned is imperfect or wanting. When the paralytic man was brought to Jesus by his four friends, it was the sight of their persevering faith which opened the way for Him, first, to pronounce his forgiveness, and then to heal him. The sick man probably caught something of the infection of his friends' faith, and certainly reaped its fruits.

So in intercession we first lift our hearts to God, and in quietness let Him strengthen again our faith in Him, and then, going out in thought to our friends, we shed around them the atmosphere, as it were, of our own faith, through which the helping, converting, or healing power of God may go forth and touch them.

This infection of the faith of others, felt through prayer, may well also strengthen the faith already possessed by those prayed for, or quicken some first sparks of it in those who as yet have none; and this will still further widen the channel along which the stream of new life can be poured.

This attempt to supply a rationale of intercession has helped to quicken my own understanding of prayer and faith in its power.

But whether or not we understand, or shall ever fully understand, the *reason* for the tremendous efficacy of prayer we may all experience the reality of the *fact*. To all of us, ordained and unordained, is committed this great priestly office and privilege of standing between God and man, and lifting holy hands of prayer 'for all estates of men', and as we pray, offering ourselves as living channels through which His life may flow forth for their healing, their direction and their strengthening.

The Prayer of Attention:

Listening

I pass now to consider a part of the morning watch to which most Christians devote far too little thought and time—the prayer of attention or listening to God. I had from earlier years realised to some extent the importance of this, particularly in connection with meditation; but I owe to my contact with the Oxford Group a much fuller understanding and use of it.

The Group has in this, as in certain other matters, not invented anything new, but rediscovered or re-emphasised a part of the Christian heritage which had fallen into the background. If prayer partakes of the nature of a conversation between ourselves and God, it must be evident that God's part in that conversation will be more important than our part, and therefore we ought to give more time to listening to God than we do to speaking to Him.

Yet is it not true that most Christians spend far *less* time in listening? As the Bishop of London, Arthur Winnington-Ingram, puts it: 'You say your prayers, but before God has time to answer you are up from your knees and off. . . . We chatter like children to their parents, and never stay to hear what the parents say. . . . It may be for years that God has been trying to say something to us, but we have never given Him time to speak to us.'

The Bible, both in the Old and the New Testament, is full of instances of God speaking to man. God speaks continually to Abraham, to Jacob, to Moses. Then, with the voice at Shiloh that answers Samuel's 'Speak, Lord, for thy servant heareth,' begins the great succession of the prophets, who constantly wait upon God to hear what He will say, and pass on His directions, warnings and encouragements to the people.

Habakkuk is typical of the prophetic outlook. 'I will stand upon my watch,' he says, 'and set me upon the tower, and will look forth to see what He will speak with me, and what I shall answer concerning my complaint. And the Lord answered me, and said, "Write the vision, and make it plain upon tablets, that he that runs may read it."'

When Ezekiel declares continually: 'The word of the Lord came to me,' he is only describing what all the prophets experienced.

When we turn to the New Testament, this prophetic note begins again. The word of God comes to John in the wilderness, and starts him on his great prophetic mission. Our Lord Himself, as we should expect, is guided all His life through by the Holy Spirit. To His disciples He promises the Holy Spirit to be their guide in all things.

Throughout the story that follows in Acts we find this happening. The Spirit fills them all at Pentecost, and takes charge of the work. He gives them the words to say, and the courage to say them, when persecution begins. He gives them definite and concrete orders from God.

Philip is sent by the desert road to Gaza, and meets with the eunuch just at the moment when he needed him. Ananias is directed to the house of Judas in Straight Street to baptise the persecutor. Saul and Barnabas are separated off by the Spirit's bidding for their work. At every step of his great missionary adventure St Paul relies on the Spirit to show him where to go and what to do.

If we would have the confident assurance of the men of the first age, the same sense of clear purpose, and the same triumphant success, we must get back to their secret of listening to God, and letting His Spirit direct. For clearly our Lord never intended nor intends that His Church should be less plainly Spirit-directed after the Apostolic age; and there have, in fact, all down its history, and not least in our own time, been multitudes of those who, through learning to listen for God's directions and obey them, have found life filled with meaning and purpose, and each day become a creative adventure for God's Kingdom.

Is it necessary for me to make clear that, when I speak of listening to God, I am not suggesting that we should expect to hear a voice with our physical ears? Such experiences are not unknown; but those mystics who have been used to hearing them are the first to depreciate their importance and give warning against undue attention to them.

No; God speaks to us not through our physical but

through our mental and spiritual faculties. Sometimes He speaks through our reason and what we call our common sense, when these are truly consecrated to Him. Sometimes He speaks through that deeper faculty of intuition, showing us things of which our ordinary reason could never have been aware. Sometimes He speaks through conscience, bringing home to us convictions of sin and challenging to new advance.

If and when God wills, He can send us sudden and unexpected directions, coming on us like a bolt from the blue. But we need not question the guidance that comes through the ordinary faculties of apprehension which He has given us. We have not to try, in listening to Him, to keep these faculties in abeyance, and 'make our minds a blank'— a feat most difficult of accomplishment! On the contrary, we should ask Him in the quietness to direct our thoughts by His Spirit, and then let our thinking have full and free range, confident that He is guiding it.

No doubt we shall make mistakes, but He can overrule them, if we are trying to do His will. No doubt, at times, our thoughts and plans may be tainted by selfish desires or impulses of which we are as yet unconscious, and which may colour or distort what God is trying to show us. But increasingly, as we grow in spiritual understanding, we shall be quick to distinguish these uprushes of self-prompted impulse from the directions of God, and our spiritual ear will grow in sure apprehension of the authentic tones of His voice.

But, if we really want in this way to receive guidance from God, there are certain conditions which we must fulfil.

We must, in the first place, be completely willing for whatever God may show us. We must, in the words of the Oxford theologian, B H Streeter, 'place ourselves without reserve at the disposal of God.' We must be unconditionally obedient to God's directions, or we must not expect any further guidance to come.

Secondly, we must be quiet and unhurried as we wait upon God—sufficiently orderly and disciplined to give ample and peaceful time. If in our time of quiet we are all the while thinking anxiously of our next job, we must not expect to hear God speak.

Lastly, we must be really out on active service in the work of the Kingdom. You cannot guide a car that is stationary; but the faster it is going, the more quickly it responds to the wheel. If we are really pledged up to the hilt to the great enterprise of winning the world to God, if our whole heart is set on it, and all our life consecrated to its achievement, then we may be sure that day by day ample directions will be given us by God about the part which He desires us to play in His great campaign.

Waiting for Orders

The prayer of attention ought, I believe, to occupy a considerable part of our morning watch with God. As I have said, it is less important to speak to God than to let Him speak to us. One way in which this prayer of attention finds scope is in listening for 'orders for the day'.

My usual practice is as follows. Having renewed my surrender to God, and told Him that I am ready for whatever He desires, and having with myself offered to Him in intercession those for whom I wish specially to pray, I then lift up before Him the day that lies ahead, and ask Him to show me His plan for it.

I can only do this because I believe that God really is interested in my day and has a plan for it. For most Christian people it is easy to believe that God in His never-failing providence holds under His direction the broad sweep of our lives, and controls its main issues. It is not always so easy to believe that He is concerned with what we call the 'small things'.

But are there really any 'small things'? And, if there are, is it possible for us to say which are small and which are great? For example, I have a choice of two planes by which to fly to India. It seems a small matter which I go by. I select one, and go by it safely. The other plane is wrecked, and all the passengers lose their lives. Was the decision, which looked so unimportant, really so? Or again, I have to go to London, and can travel by either of two equally good roads. It's a toss up which I go by. I choose one, and stop at a wayside inn for lunch. There I fall in with a man in desperate need, who confides in me, finds the solution of his trouble in God, and eventually enters the ministry of the Church, and is greatly used in the lives of multitudes of men and women. His whole future, and that of many others, has been changed by that seemingly tiny decision.

When one realises through such examples, which could be multiplied indefinitely, what great issues hang for all of us on events or decisions that appear in themselves insignificant, we realise that we must give up trying to determine what are the small things in life, and what the great. We must believe, either that the world is governed by chance, or that, if there is a divine Designer, His plan is definite and perfect in its concrete detail as well as in its broad conception and outline.

But, once this is granted, we must surely believe, further, that God can reveal to us so much of His plan as we are concerned with. If there are certain things which He desires me to do, He must be able to show me what those things are. He has made me a free agent, not a puppet in His hands. He will never, therefore, force His will upon me. He may direct and overrule many of the circumstances that surround my life, things over which I have no control. But where my own will and action are concerned, He will wait to show me His plan, longing that I on my side should be willing to learn it and co-operate in its fulfilment.

This thought of our free co-operation with God's plan carries with it two further consequences. On the one hand, we may misuse our freedom for defeating God's plan. Either we may refuse altogether to look for God's directions, preferring to plan for ourselves what we will do, or we may look for God's orders but decline to obey them.

In either of these cases we are thwarting His design; and He has then to reshape it into a new pattern, redeeming in His amazing patience what we have marred, and using for some good purpose even the mistakes which we in our wilfulness have made, if only we will at last really give our wills to Him.

But, on the other hand, if we do give Him our wills and freely co-operate with Him, then He invites us to something more than a passive acceptance of a plan He dictates to us. He invites us to share in His creative work. He is like a father who has his own ideal plan for his son's life and work in partnership with himself, and has so won his son's confidence and love that the son would trustfully and gladly accept whatever his father proposed, but who yet, out of a full and generous respect for his son's personal freedom, will not force his own plan upon him, but rather enlist the son's own creative thinking as they work out the future together. So, when we are willing to co-operate with God, we are given the amazing privilege and happiness of joint creatorship with Him. He not only lets us into His secrets and designs, calling us not servants but friends, but He even invites us to contribute to them.

We may believe, then, that God's strategy in His great campaign for winning the world is not fixed and stereotyped. It is flexible and adjustable, and that in two ways. It needs continual adjustment in face of the manoeuvres of the enemy and the failures of His own forces; and it is flexible in accepting and using any creative conception that we may contribute.

In my prayer, then, as I listen for God's orders for the day, I believe that God is interested even in so insignificant a person as myself; that He has a plan for my day, in definite and concrete detail; that my day, as He sees it, fits into His own great design, and is meant to be a day of rich and fruitful activity; and finally, that He needs my own creative thinking in planning the day with Him.

Stated in simple, practical terms, what I do myself is this. I think quietly in God's presence of the day that lies ahead. There are certain things already (under God's guidance, as I hope) planned and arranged. These I commit to Him, asking Him to show me how He would have them done, and noting any thoughts that come to me about them.

There are also the unfilled spaces of the day. I ask God to show me as much as He desires as to how He would have me spend these unoccupied times. Again I note down any thoughts that come.

I wait quietly for any other thoughts that God may give, with the desire in my heart that I may be used as fully as possible for God and His Kingdom.

Sometimes I put this desire into words in the prayer:

> *Grant me, O Lord, this day to touch as many lives as possible for Thee; and those lives do Thou by Thy Spirit quicken, whether through the words I say, the prayers I pray, the letters I write, or the life I live.*

The thoughts that come refer to all kinds of matters: letters to be written, people to be seen, things to be said, convictions to be shared, bits of work to be done.

Sometimes a fairly complete plan emerges for the day. Sometimes much of the day remains uncertain during this morning time of quiet, and becomes clear as the day goes on. Sometimes thoughts come, not simply about the day that lies ahead, but about some more remote job which has already to be taken in hand. There is no anticipating what the guidance will be. There is endless variety and delightful surprise.

I need hardly say that 'quiet times' are not restricted to the morning. The man or woman who is trying to live under God's direction will have constant momentary quiet times, and occasional longer ones, in the midst of daily work and living.

But this time of waiting upon God, morning by morning, for His directions, has given me an entirely new sense of being a man under orders, having an individual part to play in God's campaign, and under obligation to be ready and alert at His bidding.

Two things remain to be said. The first is, that I have found it an enormous help in several ways to have a notebook at hand during my times of waiting for orders, so as to write them down when they come. The main purpose of this is that I may remember them; for, as the Chinese proverb has it, 'the strongest memory is weaker than the palest ink.' But, further, unless I write what comes to me, the attempt to hold on to the first thought distracts me from being open to the next.

I have found, too, that concentration is greatly assisted by writing. So many people say: 'I find it impossible to keep my mind from wandering,' or 'My mind is a complete blank, when I seek for guidance; nothing comes.' My answer to both is, 'Try writing.'

The last word is this. If we wish to go on receiving orders from God, we must obey those that come. Let us look at our notebook later in the day (and here is a further gain from writing the orders; they cannot elude us, and slip from sight again, as they are so ready to do, particularly if they are unwelcome) and let us see that we have carried out all that we were told to do. Implicit obedience to the divine Commander is an essential attribute of a profitable soldier in His army.

Meditation

Another way by which we listen to God, and he speaks to us, is by meditation upon the Scriptures. The Bible has rightly been called the Word of God. Through it He has spoken to the hearts and minds of men all down the centuries, and still speaks. We cannot study the sayings of Christ and His disciples without realising how their minds were soaked in the Old Testament, how they drew from it continual inspiration, comfort and guidance. Nor can we read the lives of outstanding Christian men and women in all ages without discovering that constant meditation on the Bible, and particularly on the acts and words of our Lord Himself and those of His immediate followers, has played an immensely important part in shaping their thoughts and characters.

The Bible has in it *converting* power. Translated into a thousand tongues, it has been the means of leading countless men and women in all lands to their first acquaintanceship with Jesus Christ. That great Brahman convert, Narayan Vaman Tilak, owed the beginning of his spiritual pilgrimage to the New Testament given him by a courteous stranger in a railway train. He had not read further than the Sermon on the Mount before he realised that here was the Teacher for whom he had all his life been searching. He is typical of thousands.

The Bible has also power to *nourish* the new life of

the man who has turned to God. Together with the Sacraments, it is the Christian's constant food. We join ourselves in spirit to the crowd that listens to our Lord speaking from the boat on the lake, or ponder the words of St Paul as he tells us in Romans of the triumphant new life won through the Spirit of Christ Jesus, and we rise refreshed and strengthened as from a meal.

But, most of all, the Bible has power to *teach* and illumine. 'Thy Word is a lamp unto my feet, and a light unto my paths.' The Holy Spirit, who inspired the Scriptures, takes them and uses them as an instrument through which He leads us forward in the progressive understanding of God and His ways, and guides us 'into all truth'. As we meditate upon them, asking Him to teach us their meaning, we are like disciples sitting and learning at their master's feet. 'Morning by morning He wakeneth mine ear to hear, as they that are taught.' And each morning's meditation is another adventure, as we set out in exploration of 'fresh fields and pastures new'.

There are many methods of meditation, and in my opinion it is good to keep flexible in regard to method, varying it from time to time, and never allowing our practice of meditation to become formal or stereotyped.

Perhaps for most of us a perfectly simple method, with no elaborate rules or system, is the best. We open our Bible at the passage on which we are to meditate. The particular passage is decided for us either by the fact that we are working steadily through one book of the Bible, or that we are taking for meditation one of the daily lessons, or are making use of some prepared course such as that of the Bible Reading Fellowship.

The advantage of this last plan is, partly, that there are valuable notes to assist our study (though I strongly advise reading them *after* we have made a preliminary study for ourselves) and, partly, that we have the inspiration of knowing that thousands of our fellow-Christians are studying the same passage that day—including perhaps those of our own household, with whom we can then talk over later the thoughts that have come.

We ask the Holy Spirit to teach us the things He has for us to learn, and begin to read. Sundar Singh, the great Indian Christian mystic, used to advise reading through the whole passage rather rapidly first, and then starting to read it again quite slowly, verse by verse. If the passage relates to some scene which we can bring before our mind's eye (e.g. in the study of the Gospels or Acts) it is well to use all our power of imagination in visualising it. If there are phrases or verses which are difficult to understand, we must not let these distract us. We may discover the meaning of them in notes or commentary afterwards.

As we quietly read in this way, pondering each verse, and ready to learn any message which it may contain for us, it often happens that suddenly a phrase or sentence or incident leaps out, as it were, from the printed page into luminous significance. I see at once that it has a special bearing upon my own character or duty or circumstances. I realise that God is speaking to me through it, that *this* is His message to me to-day. When this happens, it is sometimes best for me to proceed no further, but concentrate on this particular message, letting it sink in deep into my mind, and trying to see any practical action which I ought to take in consequence.

But even when no such luminously clear message comes from our reading, there will always be some simple lesson to be learnt from it; and we need not be always striving after something striking or original, for it is often the old familiar truths regarding God and ourselves that we still need most to ponder and appropriate.

Once again, in connection with meditation also, let me stress the value of *writing*. Bishop Walpole of Edinburgh used to advocate writing first a paraphrase in our own words of the passage on which we are meditating, and then such thoughts as come to us about it. But in any case I would strongly recommend the practice of writing down at least such message or messages as God seems to give us through it, and particularly any conviction about some practical step which we ought to take. The advantage of this is that we may look back later, and think over again the morning's lesson, and see whether any directions that God gave us through it have been carried out.

If anyone needs a more systematic method of meditation than this very simple and informal one which I have described, I would recommend that known as the Sulpician. It applies particularly to meditations on the Gospels, and falls into three parts, described as 'Jesus before the eyes', 'Jesus in the heart', and 'Jesus in the hands'.

In the first part of our meditation we picture the scene, bringing all our powers of imagination to bear, and in particular trying to learn what special quality in our Lord's character is there portrayed. We realise more clearly, in the light of what we see in Him, our own failure in regard to this very virtue; and so, in the second part of our meditation, we open our heart to Him, and invite Him in all His sinless perfection to enter in. Finally, in the third part, we try to see how we may be the means of passing on to others something of what He gives us.

Let us suppose, for example, that I am meditating on the scene in which our Lord washes His disciples' feet. The whole incident comes vividly before my eyes, and a new realisation of His amazing humility is borne in upon me, and in the light of it my own selfish pride stands out stark and ugly. But I realise that the cure is with Him, and I invite Him to enter into my heart in all that lowly humility and by His own presence flood out the pride and self-conceit.

Lastly, I resolve to go out to others in the new spirit of humility which He brings, and I ask Him to show me where to begin—whether there is not some one person to whom I have behaved badly, and to whom I can now go in the lowliness of Christ with an apology and a desire to serve.

By such a method we may seek to grow, step by

step, into more and more of the likeness of Christ, as He more and more is given the freedom of our inmost personality.

In this chapter I have dealt entirely with meditation on the Scriptures. It only remains to be added that, while the Bible stands alone as the book for our spiritual instruction and growth, it is also of great profit at times to read and meditate upon the writings of some of the great masters of the spiritual life. Through these, too, God can speak to us, if we give Him an attentive ear.

Contemplation

WE come now to the closing moments of our morning watch with God. We have thought of the silent adoration with which we begin; the offering of our praise and thanksgiving; the renewal of our self-surrender to God's will; the lifting up before God in intercession of all those for whom we desire to pray: then the time of listening to God in the prayer of attention, as we wait for His orders for the day, and for anything that He may say to us in the quiet and as we meditate on His word.

Now, at the close of all this, and before we go out to the day's work, we must return again into the stillness, resting quietly in the presence of God, and drinking in His peace and His strength for the day's tasks.

By contemplation I mean this quiet resting in the Presence—that wonderful stillness in which we know that we are in vital touch with the living God; the stillness in which 'spirit with Spirit can meet', because

> *Closer is He than breathing,*
> *nearer than hands and feet.*

No longer are we concerned with any words or thoughts of prayer. No longer do we desire to speak to Him, nor even that He should speak to us. We desire simply to be with Him, as two lovers are content to be together without need of words.

If this book were intended for people far advanced in the spiritual life, it would be right to give a far larger place to this matter of contemplation. As Christians grow into fuller spiritual maturity and their prayer life deepens, God usually leads them to spend less time in discursive meditation, in which the mind is busily occupied with thinking, and more time in contemplation, in which this mental activity subsides and the spirit holds rapt and silent communion with God.

Some are led on beyond this state, known sometimes as 'the prayer of quiet', to the higher ranges of mystical experience, in which for a time the conscious personality itself seems almost in abeyance, and the world passes from our ken.

It is a state which William Wordsworth describes in his poem, 'Tintern Abbey':

> . . . . *that serene and blessed mood,*
> *In which the affections gently lead us on,*
> *Until, the breath of this corporeal frame*
> *And even the motion of our human blood*
> *Almost suspended, we are laid asleep*
> *In body, and become a living soul:*
> *While with an eye made quiet by the power*
> *Of harmony, and the deep power of joy,*
> *We see into the life of things.*

In India such states, which in their extreme form pass into trance and ecstasy, are studied and understood and cultivated far more fully than in the West.

Men who feel called to the life of ascetic discipline place themselves under the direction of a master *yogi* and go through the long and rigorous courses of physical, mental and spiritual training which he prescribes. In the end they undoubtedly attain to a knowledge and exercise of extraordinary psychical powers, of which the West knows little.

We practical-minded people tend to question the value of such abnormal states; but, until we understand more about them, we ought to be slow to criticise. Who can tell how much of India's mystical insight, her passionate enthusiasm for spiritual values, and her persistent rejection of materialism, is due to the spiritual force engendered by thousands of yogis constantly absorbed in contemplation of the Eternal, and from the great rampart of the northern hills continually sending out over India in prayer the infection and atmosphere of brotherly love.

Christianity also has its long succession of those who have been called to travel by the mystical way, some of whom, like the sages of India, have written systematic treatises on these more advanced stages of the spiritual life.

Christian and Hindu teaching is agreed that these higher mystical states are not for all, but are only for those whom God calls to them. Hindus would say that a man who feels he may be called to them should put himself under training and testing by an experienced *guru*. Christians would say that all should seek to go forward in the life of prayer, and should learn to practice meditation and the prayer of quiet, but that the higher mystical experiences are for those to whom God may give them. We should accept them gladly if given, but not strive after them or complain if they are withheld.

Be that as it may, I am not concerned here to do more than thus indicate the further reaches of experience to which some may find themselves called; and sometimes those of whom we would least expect it, and who would least expect it of themselves, do get called to the rarer heights of mystical experience.

But even ordinary, non-mystical Christians, for whom this book is chiefly intended, should not fail to spend at least a few minutes at the close of their morning quiet time in silent contemplation. Then, if they find the profit and help of it in any special degree, they may be led gradually on to give to it a larger and larger space in their devotions.

In these moments of contemplation, when we are still in the presence of the Lord, earth does indeed drop away out of our sight. Its cares are forgotten, its noise and bustle recede, as our spirits are lifted to serener heights. We find ourselves in a veritable Mount of Transfiguration, and we say, with Peter, 'Master, it is good for us to be here.'

For those who go often to their Communion services, this will then be the natural occasion, both for the renewal of their self-surrender, and for this specially intimate touch with the living God. But, if it is not our custom to go often, or on mornings when we do not go, it is in the last moments of the morning watch that this deep inward communion with God may be sought.

As we rest in quietness before Him, like a child reclining on its mother's breast, His peace which passes all understanding steals into our hearts to fortify them afresh against all anxiety and fear. Let us drink deep of this peace—Christ's peace, which He gives 'not as the world giveth'. From this quiet communion with Him there comes welling up in us also His deep joy that 'no man taketh away', His undiscourageable hope, His glorious selfless love.

If I have said little in this book of any prayer for ourselves and our own needs, it is because all our need is met in Christ Himself and in our ever deepening union with Him. I once heard one of my friends, who has gone far in spiritual experience, say that increasingly he had been led to turn all his petitions for personal graces and personal help into the one prayer, 'Come, Lord Jesus, and be in me all that Thou would have me be.'

And it is in those moments during which, without strain or striving, we come before Him, open unreservedly to the full inflow of His rich and glorious life, that He comes and takes possession by His Spirit, making us ever more and more completely His own, moulding us ever more and more fully by that Spirit into His own likeness.

Then, with the light of this sacred tryst with Him on the Mount still shining in our faces, and its joy in our hearts, and fortified afresh by the whole of our morning watch with God, we may go out to another day of creative work for Him in serene confidence and contagious strength.

Epilogue

SOME who read this book, or throw it aside unread, may well be inclined to regard all this talk about a morning watch as irrelevant to the real problems of the world in which we live.

Even to those who wish to be optimists the world seems, at times, to be heading for disaster. The human race, having explored the entire globe, conquered the air and eliminated space, now seems bent on annihilating itself. In such a world is there any relevance or purpose in expending so much time and energy daily on prayers and quiet times?

Perhaps it would be sufficient answer to point out that it is precisely in such a world as ours, where 'men's hearts are failing them for fear and for looking after those things that are coming on the earth,' that a secret of security and inner peace is most needed; and that, actually, the men and women whose lives are in closest touch with God are the people who possess this secret.

But there is a greater challenge. Suppose that all those who call themselves Christians were really to begin, morning by morning, to spend time with God and to listen to His orders, might not this result, not merely in ensuring their own peace of mind in the present world situation, but also in changing the whole aspect of that situation itself? If the millions who make up the membership of the Christian Church were daily available to God and under His direction, can we doubt that in a comparatively short time the nations would be brought under His control, and a new and a better world would be born?

For the world's present need, God, and God alone, has the answer. We have been desperately unwilling to recognise this; but by tragic experience of every other way the truth is being forced home upon us. What, then, might not God do if the whole Christian Church were awake and listening to Him and prepared to obey His will—a disciplined army under His command? What might not happen? The disappearance of fear, hatred, antagonism, war. A new world order. Human life remade.

Is there, then, no relevance in listening to God? Is it not the one thing most needed? And if so, will I, at any cost, do my part?